A VIEW FROM BELOW

A View From Below

A NEW YORK CITY TRANSIT EMPLOYEE'S ACCOUNT OF SEPTEMBER 11, 2001

Steven McEnearney

Sharon Ink Productions, LLC

Copyright © 2021 Steven McEnearney

All Rights Reserved.
No part of this book may be used or reproduced by any means, graphic, electronic, or mechanical, including photocopying, recording, taping, or by any information storage retrieval system without the written permission of the copyright owner, except in the case of brief quotations embodied in critical articles and reviews.

To request permissions, contact Steven McEnearney at sharonmcenearney@squigglesbysharon.com

Paperback: ISBN 978-1-7368318-2-3
Ebook: 978-1-7368318-3-0

Proudly published by:
Sharon Ink Productions, LLC

Printed by IngramSpark in the USA

*September 11, 2001 was a day that changed America.
That morning, Steven McEnearney, a train service supervisor for
the New York Transit Authority,
went to work like it was any other day.
He could not have imagined what
that day would end up becoming.
This is his story, in his own words, unedited.*

Hi, my name is Steve. On September 11, 2001 I was a Train Service Supervisor for the New York City Transit Authority. Today is September 10, 2020, and it's 1:30 a.m. I'm retired, and I can't sleep. I feel compelled to attempt to finish my account of what occurred to me on that fateful day 19 years ago. It has taken me years to write my account. Every time I attempt write, I can only write so much before becoming overwhelmed. So I put it away for 6 months, a year, try again, put it away, you get the picture. I started writing in late September of 2001, and here I am all these years later. The events of my day on September 11, 2001 play though my mind, over and over, clear as day, every second of it. It's not there all the time, but when it is, it reels out in my memory as if it were yesterday.

A Train Service Supervisor's job involves many aspects. Making sure that the men and women that actually operate the trains are complying with the rules and regulations pertaining to their jobs is the main priority. The other main aspect is responding to any and all reported situations, emergencies, signal failures, derailments, collisions, customer injuries and fatalities; coordinating the response between NYCT and the NYPD, FDNY, EMS and any other agency required to resolve the situation. Pretty much handling just about anything that comes along. The train crews and the Train Service Supervisors are the eyes and ears of the subway system. So with that said, here's my account of September 11, 2001, a different view from below the streets of NYC.

My day began as any other day; I was assigned to cover the Times Square area on the 7th Avenue, 1, 2, 3 subway lines from 6am till the end of rush hour. The morning was going smoothly until I heard a radio transmission from a number 1 train that was at the World Trade Center station, headed towards South Ferry. The Train Operator was reporting passengers holding the doors open on the train. Seconds later there were reports of gunfire in the station. I started monitoring the situation more closely. The next thing I heard was another radio report from a subway Car Maintainer on duty at the Chambers Street Station. He was reporting an explosion in the World Trade Center. The two reports were conflicting but I knew where I was. I boarded the next Brooklyn bound number 2 train, informed my Rail Control Center Dispatcher that I was in route to the problem, and unknowingly headed into the worst day of my life. I arrived at Chambers St. about 12 minutes later.

On the way downtown, I spoke with the Train Operator, and monitored the radio. As we were speaking, the Rail Control Center reported that a plane had struck the World Trade Center. Being underground, unable to see what was happening, both the Train Operator and I speculated that a small plane, like a piper cub, must have inadvertently crashed into the building. It seemed to me, unbelievable, that a pilot could have not seen a building that big.

When I arrived at Chambers Street, I was totally unprepared for what I was about to see. Exiting the train I saw the subway Car Maintainer that reported the explosion. I approached him, he was just standing there with a look of shock on his face, all he could said was, "you have to go up to the street and see the fucking hole in the building" Nothing could have prepared me for what I was about to see and experience for the next 12 hours.

Walking up the subway stairs was nearly impossible, people were running, screaming crying, and scared. Arriving at the top of the stairs I looked up at the Tower in front of me, a hole from the west edge of the north tower to the east edge of the building, up high, near the top, shaped like a jet plane as if looking at it from behind. The flames and black smoke were billowing out of that enormous hole. I could hear the sound of the flames, almost a boiling sound. If you've ever heard gasoline burning, you know what I mean. Unable to comprehend what I was seeing, I thought, how the hell did the pilot not see that building? What was wrong with the air traffic controllers? What the hell happened? Terrorism didn't even enter my mind. I looked again, there were people all along the jagged bottom edge of the plane shaped hole in the building, flames and smoke silhouetted them. They were waving things around, trying to get someone's, anyone's attention, and they were throwing things out of the hole, the fire raging behind them. It was then I realized they weren't throwing things. They were falling out of the building, after leaning out as far as they could to escape the flames. They were being forced out by the smoke and fire. Others were standing at the edge of the hole for a second then just jumped, knowing their fate was sealed. I was shocked and horrified by the sight, frozen in place by it, trying to understand it. I couldn't seem to look away.

I saw movement from the corner of my eye, I heard the collective gasp of the crowd. I turned my head. I watched as the second jet punctured the other tower, the seconds ticked out like an eternity, then the fireball blasted out of the other side of the building, raining fire, debris and death down on the street below. Once again I was horrified, and thought, what the hell is wrong with the air traffic controllers? Terrorism again did not cross my mind. My brain didn't comprehend what I was seeing; it was trying to rationalize it, trying to figure out a logical reason for what I was seeing.

I heard a little girl screaming "Daddy" The voice pulled me from what I was looking at. I turned to see her pointing at the blazing towers; she was holding her mother's hand. The mother just looked at me and stated as a matter of fact that the little girls' daddy worked in the towers. I don't know why I did what I did next. Maybe it was because I have three daughters of my own. I knelt down, looked her in the eyes, and told her that I was sure her daddy was ok, not to worry. I don't know to this day if it was a lie or the truth, but I couldn't look at that child, who was so upset and do nothing. The mother looked at me and started leading the girl away, towards the corner, getting ready to cross the street and go. I was behind them, the mother and daughter took one step off the curb. I saw movement from the corner of my eye. I saw a city bus, commandeered by the Police. It was racing down the street, hell bent on getting to the towers. It wasn't going to stop. I reached out and pulled the mother and daughter back to the sidewalk as the bus, never slowing went past them, not one foot from the curb.

I think I was in shock because I found myself trying to direct the traffic in that intersection, trying to make order out of chaos, then more police arrived took control of the area. In a sort of daze I headed back down into the subway, my head reeling, I knew I had work to do. Standing on that corner; seeing the things I'd seen seemed like an eternity, but in actuality it had all happened very quickly. Rational thought would have to wait; there was a lot to be taken care of in the subway. My day had just begun.

As I walked back down to the subway platform my mind was reeling, my priority now was the safety of the customers and train crews. Organizing my thoughts I set about doing just that. Arriving at the Chambers Street platform I ordered the next South Ferry bound number 1 train to stop and stay in the station, feeling it was unsafe for service to proceed directly under the World Trade Center. I called the Times Square tower and instructed them to let the train reverse direction and start heading back uptown. At this point it seemed the safest choice, but I was met with opposition from the Rail Control Center. They were ordering me over the radio to let the service continue through to South Ferry. I couldn't believe that they wanted to try to send trains though the area. I told the Train Operator, under no circumstances was he to move that train until I came back. As this was happening I had hundreds of customers asking me what was happening, what they should do, what alternate service they could use, and why was I not letting the train go through. I just told them that the World Trade Center was burning and it would be in their best interest to go home, and not to work today. It was chaos, everything happening at the same time. I bet no one ever told them to go home before, some took the warning, and some did not. I went to the phone and called the Rail Control Center and told them there was no way on earth that subway service should or would continue while I was on the scene and in charge. I fought with them and basically told them that they had no way to know how bad things truly were on the street above. I was taking full responsibility for my decision, just let me handle it. With that call I'm guessing I saved some lives. The service was rerouted to other places, but one problem still remained. There was still a train at the South Ferry station waiting to head back uptown. I radioed that train and instructed them to pick up as many people as they could at Rector Street and World Trade Center and then get that train out of there. The train crew complied and did as told; they were the last train through that area for a long time afterwards.

After the train cleared the area, my direct manager arrived on scene. He took a quick run upstairs, and came back looking a few years older. We decided that now that service was safely redirected we should check to make sure that the World Trade Center station was fully evacuated and that the entrances and exits were closed and locked. Leaving from the Chambers Street station we proceeded to walk along the tracks towards the World Trade Center station. We climbed up onto the World Trade Center platform, and began checking for customers, making sure it was locked up and in a short time determined that it was secured. We had a quick conversation about what to do next, walk back to Chambers Street on the tracks or exit to the street above and then walk back. We decided that even though the building was burning, we would walk through the mezzanine where the stores were and exit to the street, then make our way to wherever we were needed. That decision almost cost us our lives.

As we walked into the lower level of the World Trade Center where the stores were, we were met with the smell of jet fuel, smoke, and a lot of water. There were a number of emergency personnel tending to the injured and burned people. They were breaking open the store fronts to get to bottled water to pour over the people. I looked to my left and an elevator door opened and more injured people and fire department personnel came out. There were so many people on stretchers, on counters, in chairs, all over, injured, being triaged, but most of them were alive. We continued to make our way towards the non-working escalators; climbing to the top we could see daylight again. There were a lot of loud sounds we kept hearing, thudding, things falling, hitting the street, the building, and the overhangs on the building.

Arriving at the doors that led to the street we were met by the police, they told us we would be safer inside the building as parts of the planes, the buildings and bodies were falling in the street right outside the door. I looked at my manager and he looked at me, someone else approached the exit door and the police turned their attention to them. Without a word both my manager and I took advantage of the police officers distraction pushing our way through the doors and onto the street. The officer realizing what we were doing shouted for us to stop, but we didn't.

Once on the street we realized the enormity of the situation. There was the front landing gear of one plane, the jet engine, unrecognizable twisted chunks of metal and bodies, some covered, some not. We proceeded towards the corner. Stepping off the curb I glanced to my right, there sitting on the curb next to a mail box was a woman; she was burned from head to toe and looked a red as a lobster. We locked eyes, hers pleading for help, I felt her eyes burning into my soul. I hope she made it, I couldn't stop, I couldn't stop, there was too much debris falling around us. I don't know if the woman lived or died, I hope she understood that I couldn't help her, the danger was all surrounding, I had to keep going.

The buildings around the World Trade Center were on fire, windows were blowing out spraying glass, flames pouring out of every window. The debris was falling, and people were running. I remember feeling the heat. It seemed that the whole world was turning upside down, burning. I looked back for my manager and he had stopped in the middle of the street. Standing there with all hell falling from the sky, he was frozen, looking up taking pictures. I couldn't believe it, he was stopping to take pictures, frozen, lost in the moment, risking his life for what? He didn't seem to realize the danger that surrounded him. I yelled to him, we have to get the fuck out of here! He turned and looked at me, seeming to wake up, breaking the trance that held him stationary. He snapped out of his trance, and he began running toward me. Together we ran up the block away from the devastation that surrounded us.

Further up the block was the entrance to the Fulton Street subway, a major transfer point within the subway system. We hurtled down the stairs towards safety, but safety was a relative term on that day. We ran into the mezzanine level near the token booth and stopped. A woman approached us holding a two year old boy, she was asking us what to do, where to go. It was in the middle of her second question when her face dropped, her question stopped and her mouth hung open, she was speechless looking as if she had seen a ghost, and pointing over my shoulder.

I spun around to see what she was pointing at, that's when I saw it. A tremendous wall of boiling beige smoke was rolling and boiling directly at us, before I could say anything it enveloped us, everything disappeared in a cloud of smoke and dust. I pulled my t-shirt up over my face and told the woman to cover her and the boy's face. At that point all hell was breaking loose and I lost sight of my manager, he had run when he saw the smoke, I stayed put. I just could not leave that woman and child alone to fend for themselves. They say when an emergency happens people will do one of two things, either take flight, or stand and fight, I choose the latter without even realizing it. Suddenly some firefighters ran down the stairs into the subway station, they saw me wearing my safety vest and said, "you're the subway guy, what do we do?" I honestly thought there had been an explosion in the subway. I also thought that we were screwed if they were asking me what to do. I did not know the first tower had fallen.

Based on my assumption of a subway explosion I figured smoke rises, so I said follow me and we went down to the deepest point in the station. On the way down more customers began to appear as the dust was beginning to settle and visibility got a bit better. By the time we got all the people down into the lowest level of the station there was around 50-75 people in the group. The firefighters wanted to walk the train tracks to the next station to get away from the dust. I knew that couldn't be done because I didn't know if the trains were still running in the area or if the third rail was still live. It was too dangerous of an option. I tried to call the Rail Control Center to get information and direction, but the Rail Control no longer was able to respond, the radio was useless.

I told everyone to wait on the platform while I went back upstairs to see if the smoke and dust had cleared and to find a safe way out, all the gates were locked and the station was now abandoned. Finally, I found a gate that was unlocked and went to the street, all I could see was the subway entrance globe. I then returned to the people I had left downstairs. Knowing now that there wasn't an explosion in the subway, I led the group back up and out of the station. As we were leaving someone said they saw people going into a room near the exit, I knocked on the door and someone opened it. Inside was another group of people including a blind man and his guide dog. I escorted them out also. As we approached the exit by the token booth, there was a man lying on the ground, he was saying he had chest pains and had a heart condition. I along with another person helped him up and carried him to the street, where by a small miracle there was an ambulance. I knocked on the door and it opened, there were what looked like 8 to 10 people inside, he made eleven, I slammed the door closed, tapped on it twice and it pulled away. The people I led out of the subway had now disappeared, I was standing in the middle of the street by myself, the smoke and dust was settling, the dust and debris was now ankle deep on the ground.

Standing there wondering what to do next, groups of dust covered people began approaching from all directions asking what they should do, they were lost and disoriented. I started directing them towards the Brooklyn Bridge thinking they should try to get the hell out of Manhattan before something else happened. I stood there directing people until they stopped coming, then headed towards the Brooklyn Bridge myself, but I didn't make it. I saw a cell phone store with the front security gate half closed; I ducked under it, opened the door and went inside. The man who owned the store allowed me to use the bathroom to wash some of the dust off. While there I took my T-shirt off and made it into some facemasks to tie around my nose and mouth. They also let me use the phones that were working. I contacted my Rail Control Center and informed them of my location, it was then I learned that one of the towers had fallen. I was instructed to check the subway tracks between Fulton Street and Wall Street for damage, stuck trains, lost passengers and crew members. I wasn't able to contact my family in New Jersey, but I was able to speak to my Mother-in-law in Staten Island and let her know I was ok, and told her to call home.

As I hung up the phone a group of about six firefighters entered the store and slammed the door behind them, the widows suddenly turned dark with beige dust and you could not see outside. This new cloud of dust was from the second tower falling. We waited until most of the dust cleared and with my makeshift dust mask we ventured back outside, the firefighters went back towards what was later called the pile. I went back to the subway as instructed.

My job now was to make sure there were no trains in the downtown area that were trapped with people on them. Going back into the subway at Fulton Street was surreal, covered in dust ankle deep, empty. I'd never seen the subway completely empty, abandoned, as if the world had ended and I was the only survivor. Many subway lines converge at Fulton St. I began by first checking all the platforms, and corridors, but found no people or trains. I then started walking the #2 & #3 downtown subway tracks from Fulton St. towards Park Place and Wall St checking both the Uptown and Downtown tracks. During my walk I found 13 600ft subway trains and checked each and every one to make sure there were no customers trapped, and to make sure they were properly secured and would not roll away if power was lost. I thanked God that the 13 crews that were on those trains had took it upon themselves to evacuate their customers safely and properly secured their equipment before heading to safety themselves.

As I was walking through the abandoned train, I heard a radio transmission from an Uptown train that was sitting in the Wall St. station. The Train Operator was talking to the tower trying to get the signal for him to reverse direction and go back to Brooklyn. I thought if I could reach Wall St. before he pulled out I could finally get away from the dust and destruction. I tried to call the Train with my radio, but received no response. I hurried my step and as I climbed up on the dust covered Wall St. platform all I saw was the trains' tail lights as it pulled away and disappeared into the tunnel. Wondering what to do next, I continued to walk along the platform. As I reached the middle of the platform another Uptown train pulled in, I couldn't believe my eyes. Again I thought here's my chance to get out of here, but I was wrong again.

I waited for the Train Operator to walk back to the downtown end of the train and identified myself. We boarded the train and got it ready to move back to Brooklyn. Then we waited, and waited. The crew and I used our radios and tried calling the Rail Control Center, and the tower that controlled the switches and signals to request clearance to move back to Brooklyn but received no response. After another short period of waiting I walked to an emergency phone located on the tunnel wall and called the tower. When the Tower Operator answered the phone, he told me that the Police had given instructions that no further trains would be allowed through the under river tunnels until further notice. We were now stuck in Manhattan at Wall St., the Train Operator, the Conductor and I.

We sat on that train and waited, I gave them pieces of my T-shirt to use as dust masks, we turned off the air condition on the train as the train began to fill with dust. It was hot and eerily quiet. After a while we decided to secure the train and see if we could find a safer place to wait until we received further instruction from the Rail Control Center. We went upstairs to the street and we saw the Regent Hotel, so we went inside, figuring if we were stuck in Manhattan we might as well check it out. On 9/11 the Regent was supposed to be hosting a business meeting and luncheon, obviously it didn't happen. Instead they had refugees seeking shelter from the terrorist attack all solemnly sitting in the fully set up ballroom. The staff of the hotel let us wash up and gave us food and soda. They also let us use the phones to call family and the Control Center. I couldn't thank them enough. The large screen TV's in the Ballroom showed the building falling again and again. They showed the President being notified as he read books to children. I couldn't believe my eyes. Somehow I had lived through that.

I telephoned the Rail Control Center and was instructed to check the trains every hour or so, which I did twice. When reporting back my findings after the second inspection of the equipment I was told that a water main break had been reported at the Rector St station on the #1 line and was ordered to go check and report back.

As I walked across town to reach Rector St., I ran into some construction workers who saw my t-shirt dust mask. They asked me if I wanted a real mask, and of course I said yes. After a short wait they came back out of the building they were working on and gave me three dust masks, one for me, one for the Train Operator, and one for the Conductor waiting back at the hotel. I continued my walk towards what is now called ground zero. I observed Manhattan as I'd never seen it before, dust coated everything and it was six inches deep on the sidewalks. It was totally silent and every sound was muffled like after a heavy snowstorm. The sky was the same color as the dust and the sun looked like a lamp behind a curtain. There was no one on the street except me. The Traffic lights continued to change for the non-existent traffic and still I looked both ways before crossing. As I approached the next intersection I saw a man walking towards me, he was dressed in hospital scrubs and carried a medical bag. As he approached he spoke to me. He told me that he was a doctor, I don't remember from what hospital. He said he went to the World Trade Center to help. He said when he arrived there was no one to help. He said they were all dead. Then he shrugged his shoulders and kept walking.

As I started walking again I thought about the enormity or what he said. I thought about how many people must have died.

Those two buildings were the tallest buildings in the world for a while, there must have been thousands and thousands inside. What about the people around them on the ground, emergency responders. The number and the magnitude of this disaster began to settle into my mind, how many could have died? 10 thousand, 20?

When I finally reached Rector St. there were firemen near the entrance to the station. I asked them if they knew anything about a water main break. They looked at me like I was crazy, and looking back I must have been, considering what was had happened and what was now going on a few blocks to the North. To be concerned about a water main break was ridiculous, to be checking for it was even crazier. Then again I was given instructions and I had my job to do and the firemen had there's. I turned on my flashlight and descended into the Rector St. station to check. It was pitch black down inside the station, if you've ever experienced total darkness you'll know exactly how dark it was. I walked the platform, then descended to the tracks and continued walking towards the World Trade Center station where this whole adventure had begun earlier. Everything was creaking and moaning as I walked. I saw movement up ahead and shined my flashlight in that direction. My light lit up an orange reflectorized vest, and I saw a man who was contracted by NYCT to perform some job in the tunnel. He was just wandering around in the pitch black with no flashlight looking for his partners. I lead him out to the street at the Rector St. station, He was very disoriented, confused, and upset because his co-workers were missing. I don't know how long he was down there in the dark but I would guess for hours, he was lucky he wasn't killed or seriously hurt. Once back on the street I found an ambulance and put him in it. I don't know what became of him, or if he found his friends. I didn't find a water main break. A few hours later I learned that the very tunnel I had walked in had collapsed and the WTC station had been destroyed by the collapse of the towers. I guess I was blessed that day.

Back on the street I began walking toward the World Trade Center I found a pay phone that was bent over and covered with dust, but still working. Finally I was able to contact my family, they were very relived, and still very concerned for my safety. Hanging up the phone I continued my walk, what I saw was beyond description, The dust coated everything, cars were spun around, upside down, crashed into one another, burning, up on sidewalks, into buildings, scattered about and left in a hurry. It was every disaster movie ever made, live right before my eyes. As I neared the intersection where the Towers once stood, there was a little park, with a statue of a man sitting on a bench with his suitcase. That park was devastated, The tops of the trees were sheared off, trees were laying over like a tsunami hit them, blown over away from the WTC site. A very tall scaffold, perhaps 40-50 stories that was once attached to the building near it was lying in a heap like a scattered erector set, and there was fire everywhere. The only thing left standing in that park was the statue of the man sitting with the suitcase.

Standing on that corner, I turned around and surveyed the scene, the buildings were all damaged. They all had broken windows, and facades, many were ablaze, they had holes in them from the debris blasted at them when the towers imploded. It was all so surreal just standing there looking at what remained, looking at the pile of rubble that was once one of the tallest building in the world. Fingers of the façade of the WTC were sticking up towards the sky, some 20 stories or more tall. Paper was floating down, on fire they burned as they hit the ground, like a ticker tape parade gone horribly wrong. All sound was muffled from the depth of the dust. Firefighters were breaking out the windows and windshields of the burnt and damaged fire trucks so they could be driven, many were just walking around in a daze. Police and other responders were just trying to comprehend the situation. The sun was like a yellow disk in a dust and smoke filled sky, I imagined that this must be what its like after a nuclear explosion. The sounds I heard were not those of people crying out for help, this situation was beyond that.

I heard the sounds of the sirens of the emergency vehicles trying to sound from under the rubble, it was a warped futile sound. I also heard the sounds of the beeping devices that firemen wear to alert others that they have fallen or are incapacitated. As I continued to walk past the remains of the towers I saw the lives of many of the WTC's occupants spread all over the area. There were pictures with burnt edges, computer monitors, little knick knacks that people must have had on their desks, hand bags, articles of clothing, shoes, briefcases, hats, and other assorted objects. I don't think I've ever felt so much hopelessness and despair in my life.

Still walking north I saw the Borders bookstore that I had run past on my way out of the North tower before it fell, it was still fully ablaze, uncontrolled, the heat baking at me as I passed by.

Eventually I made my way back to the Regent Hotel, called the Rail Control Center and reported that there wasn't a water main break at Rector St. and that I was back in the hotel with the train crew I had left there. I checked in with the Rail Control Center periodically and watched the big screen TV's replay the days events over and over. Sometime later, realizing that the crew wouldn't be needed, I gave the crew the dust masks I was given and told them to go home however they could, they walked North towards the safe zone that was established around 14th St. as some limited subway service was available there.

Shortly after when I called the Rail Control Center again they told me I could go home. I wasn't sure what to do at that point, all bridges and tunnels were closed, no public transportation was available and I lived in New Jersey. As I walked north towards the Brooklyn Bridge, I planned on walking to Brooklyn, and then try to get to Staten Island to my mother in-laws house. Along the way I found that the SeaStreak Ferry that runs between lower Manhattan and the Atlantic Highlands in New Jersey was shuttling people from Manhattan to Brooklyn and then going back to New Jersey. I headed to the South Street Seaport. I arrived at the seaport around 7 p.m. and the crew let me come aboard, they weren't charging anyone a fare, so I thanked them and found a seat. There was only one problem with my escape from NY plan, the fact of the matter was that this ferry would drop me off in New Jersey many miles from where my car was parked in a park and ride lot.

After the ferry stopped in Brooklyn to let people off and more people on the boat set sail and proceeded across NY harbor, passing under the Verrazano-Narrows Bridge, and out along the coast of Staten Island. All the while I was just sitting looking off the back of the boat at the NY City skyline, forever changed. The dust cloud had pretty much settled, but the thick column of black smoke from the uncontrolled fires rose high into the sky and stretched out over Brooklyn and then out over the Atlantic ocean.

I was tired, dirty, dusty, and heartsick over what I had seen and by what I was still seeing. While on the boat I met a group of people that worked uptown, they asked me about what had happened, what I had seen, what I had experienced, and what I had done. I told them the short version of what had transpired during my day, they just sat and listened. When I got to the end of my story they were just sitting there, mouths slightly open, staring at me. I told them I didn't know how I was going to get home once we got to NJ and about my car being parked miles away from the drop off point. Then one of the guys I was talking to told me that his car was in the same parking lot as mine. I was actually stunned when he said that, of all the people I could have run into, I met him, it was really quite amazing to me. I don't remember his name, but he told me that his brother was going to pick him up and that he would give me a ride back to my car, I was floored. I was never more thankful to a stranger for a favor in my life.

When the boat docked it was met by the NJ State Police and Fire Department personnel. As the people on board were walking off, the authorities were dividing us up into two groups. Those that were covered in dust and those that weren't. I was still covered in dust and dirt and the people I met onboard the boat were not, we were split up. I thought oh well, there goes my ride. After being separated I had to walk through a plastic lined ditch filled with water. Then I was told to stand in front of a railing and the firemen hosed me down. I was given a white paper suit, I changed into it in a port-o-san, then, I dumped my wet clothes into a dumpster. The dusty people were then sent to a corralled area where I was identified, and interviewed by various law enforcement agencies. They asked all the who, what, where, when questions and then sent me out to where the rest of the people were trying to get rides home, or were boarding busses.

It took about an hour to get off the boat and through the corralled area, I figured I would have to find my own way home at this point. Much to my surprise, the guy I had met on the boat and the people he was with were waiting for me, and waved to get my attention as I walked out into the parking lot. I felt like crying, they could have left over an hour ago, but they waited for me, a total stranger. To this day I still feel like crying whenever I think about the kindness of those people.

They led the way to a white Chrysler Minivan and we all piled in, a short while later I was in my car at the park n ride near my home. I couldn't believe they waited for me, I hope somehow they know how much that meant to me. Ten minutes later I was pulling into my driveway, it was just around 11 p.m.

My wife met me at the front door, she had put down newspaper from the front door, up the stairs and into the bathroom. She handed me a plastic bag and into the shower I went. After I retraced my steps back to the front door picking up the paper and bagging it as I went out the front door to the garbage pail.

I was exhausted, and my breathing was heavy from the dust, so I got back into the car and went to the emergency room. I was treated and after a while sent home. Once back home I called my work Rail Control Center and informed them that I wouldn't be back at work for a few days and filed an on the job injury form for good measure, just in case I got sick from the incident, 19 yrs. later I'm still doing ok.

I returned to work about six days later, where I was assigned to the Chambers St. station for the a.m. rush hour. The station had been cleaned and hosed down but it was still very dusty. We had to change the air conditioner filter at least 2 times a day and still we were coughing. There was also a burning stench that permeated the station. I spent a few months down there until I was able to select another work location, outside on the #7 line. During those months I walked down to the WTC a few times and watched as they dug through the debris, it was very sad.

On that day many innocent people tragically lost their lives, and I'm sorry for their loss. Fire fighters, and Police and many other agencies tragically lost many of their members. They acted heroically, selflessly, and died tragically. I'm sorry for their loss also. I would never, nor would I intentionally dishonor their valor or their sacrifice. They were heroes.

The whole WTC attack was a horrendous day for everyone. In the aftermath and in the months following the attack a small trivial thing began to bother me. It was politically incorrect to talk about so we kept our mouths shut. It's something many people never gave a second thought about. It was never really recognized or talked about by elected officials, the media, or the public.

It was the fact that the employees of NYC Transit acted heroically also. Yet no one ever acknowledged it. My story is only one of hundreds of stories that you never heard and probably never will. Transit workers just get it done and keep on moving.

In actuality, thousands of citizen's lives were probably saved on 9/11 by the actions of transit employees. There's no way to actually know how many lives were saved because, the fact is we were the only city agency in which not one customer and not one employee died as a result of the actual attack. We didn't realize it at the time, and it didn't matter, we were just doing our jobs

I know that we didn't rush into the burning buildings, but we were there, under them as they burned, in the subway, redirecting trains away from the area, making sure the stations under the WTC were cleared of people and securing them, moving people away from the danger. While the towers were burning we were still running trains around them.

When the towers fell, we were right there under them as they came down. In the stations and in the tunnels, not knowing what was happening above us. The WTC station on the one line collapsed and the tunnel between WTC and Rector St, collapsed a few hours later. All we knew was that an attack had occurred on our city and we were doing everything we could to get everyone we could to safety.

Train crews all over the downtown area evacuated thousands of customers from packed, stalled, rush hour trains. Without regard for their own safety, under the worst possible conditions, with little to no visibility, and with no available communication with authorities they lead people to safety.

A little known fact, after the towers fell, NYCT responded to the scene before the day was halfway through. Transit employees and equipment were initially staged in Brooklyn. Then a caravan of vehicles of every type and description, and hundreds of Transit workers, of every skilled trade drove over the Brooklyn Bridge and descended on the WTC site. They were equipped with heavy equipment, dump trucks, excavators, backhoes, tractors cranes, welders, cutters, pumps, hoses, and every type of equipment needed for a search and rescue. After the buildings came down, they were the first responders, arriving before the military.

These Transit workers cleared the streets surrounding the WTC of vehicles and debris so the military could reach the site without delay, they climbed on the pile of burning wreckage and started cutting away metal, breaking away concrete, digging for what they hoped would be survivors, they worked even after the military arrived, they worked on their days off, bucket after bucket of debris, yet they received no mention in the paper, there was no mention of them by the officials.

Many of those that worked there during the search and rescue and then on the recovery, and then on the rebuilding of the subway tunnels got sick from their time there, many have died of these illnesses, never seeing a retirement check. NYCT employees were heroes also.

It took me almost twenty years to complete this writing, it was hard. I'd start and become overwhelmed, close the note book and walk away, so each segment is written with years of time in between. My story is finally done. I'm still surviving; the nightmares have faded, but return from time to time. Whenever a plane flies over I look up, loud noises startle me. Younger people that say get over it have no idea what those there that day experienced, they make me angry. I will NEVER FORGET and I WILL NEVER FORGIVE those responsible for the attacks on the World Trade Center.

EYEWITNESS TO TRAGEDY

Almost 3,000 people are missing, dead or presumed dead in the terrorist attack against the World Trade Center. This unthinkable tragedy has gripped the nation and life as we knew prior to September 11, 2001 will never be the same. Miraculously, thousands escaped with their lives, although, many sustained injuries. In a moving and compelling account of this unimaginable event, a member of the RTO family poignantly describes what it was like to be at the Twin Towers when it became the latest Ground Zero. Here is his story.

On the morning of September 11, I was on duty at Times Square, when I heard a radio transmission of a shooting at Cortlandt Street in the World Trade Center. Moments later, I heard another radio transmission reporting an explosion at the same location.

I quickly boarded a Brooklyn-bound train and got off at Chambers Street, went to the street above and observed the twin towers with gaping holes and flames. I helped clear the street for emergency vehicles until police arrived. Once back in the subway, I met Superintendent **James Ferebee** and we walked the tracks to reach Cortlandt Street to make sure there were no customers in the station. After finding no one, we walked through the Trade Center's concourse and exited at Church Street.

While outside, we were told by emergency workers to stay under the building's ledge, as there was falling debris. Feeling unsafe there, we dashed along Fulton Street until reaching Broadway where we noticed customers exiting the subway in an area where debris was falling. Quickly, we went into the subway to direct the customers away from this perilous location. Next we discovered about 100 customers in a passageway and directed them to a safe area to exit.

Suddenly, there was a loud boom as the first tower had fallen, seven minutes after we had left the building. A wall of white smoke and dust blasted through the Broadway-Nassau/Fulton Street complex. Superintendent Ferebee and I became separated.

Customers began panicking and I told them to use whatever they had to cover their faces, to remain calm and stay put. I went to the street and amazingly you could not see your hand in front of your face. The only thing visible was the illuminated globe on top of the staircase. I went back in the subway and led the customers through the dust to the lowest level of the station complex.

Returning to street level and finding that visibility had improved, I went back into the subway to get the customers and led them to the street. A woman approached me and told me a group of people were in a storage room. She led the way and I found about five people, including a visually impaired man and his guide dog. I led this group to safety.

While walking towards Brooklyn Bridge station, I stopped at a cellular phone store and the owner was kind enough to let me use the telephone to call the Subways Control Center. As I was on the telephone, the second tower fell and again the entire area was enveloped with gray-white powder. I waited for the dust to subside and then went to Fulton Street on the Lexington Avenue line to check for customers. I found none.

I met a train crew that had secured their train at the Fulton Street station. We walked to the Regent Wall Street Hotel at Wall and William Streets where the hotel management let us use the telephone to contact Control Center.

After waiting for several hours, Control Center directed me to go Rector Street station to check a report of a water main break and a tunnel collapse. I walked through the station and found everything intact and no sign of a watermain break. I then went to the site where the World Trade Center had stood for almost 30 years.

The destruction was beyond anything I can describe. Trees in the park were blown over and the tops were sheared off. Dust and debris was everywhere-including on people. Fire trucks and other emergency vehicles were crushed and ablaze. Numerous fire trucks were driving around with missing windshields. I simply could not believe what I was seeing. Disheartened, I returned to the hotel where I reported my findings at Rector Street to Control Center

Once instructed to go home, I walked to the South Street Seaport and caught a ferry to New Jersey. As I left New York, I began coughing and my throat was burning. I viewed a skyline that would never be the same: black smoke was rising and visible for miles. I had been spared from being crushed when the first tower collapsed by a mere seven minutes.

Although, I helped as many people as I could, I only wished I could have done more. I did my best, yet it doesn't feel like I did enough. The enormity of what happened began to sink in.

When the ferry docked in New Jersey, a Hazardous Material unit from the Atlantic Highlands Fire Department met me. They told me that airborne asbestos particles were in the air over Lower Manhattan and I was instructed to stand against a fence and be watered down by a blast from a fire hose. I was given a paper jumpsuit, and told to change into it, and throw away my clothing. Because I continued to cough, I went to Bayshore Hospital. I was treated for smoke and dust inhalation and airborne asbestos. I was given prescriptions for an inhaler and antibiotics and then released.

The following day I saw my personal physician and was told to return to work on Monday, September 17. Sadly, this event has forever changed my life.

● Train Service Supervisor
Steven R. McEnearney

Steven's original account of the 9/11 attacks written for a NYCT news bulletin
Steven McEnearney

Steven McEnearney was a NYCT employee the day of the September 11th attacks. He continued to work as a train service supervisor and retired in 2015. He lives in NJ with his partner, Donna, and their dog, Freddy. Steve has a passion for refurbishing vintage cars.

Steven with his refurbished 1965 Pontiac Tempest Station Wagon
Steven McEnearney

CPSIA information can be obtained
at www.ICGtesting.com
Printed in the USA
BVHW041008161121
621763BV00014B/341